Living With Purpose

WORKBOOK

A Framework for Igniting Your Fullest Potential

Copyright © 2023 by Michelle Hubert

Published by Korsgaden Insights

All rights reserved. No portion of this book may be reproduced, stored in a retrieval system, or transmitted in any form or by any means—electronic, mechanical, photocopy, recording, scanning, or other—except for brief quotations in critical reviews or articles, without prior written permission of the author.

For foreign and subsidiary rights, contact the author.

Cover design by Sara Young
Cover Photo by Amy Jaacks amyjaacksphotography.com (front cover)
Andrew van Tilborgh (back cover)

ISBN: 978-1-959095-49-1   1 2 3 4 5 6 7 8 9 10

Printed in the United States of America

MICHELLE HUBERT

Living With Purpose
WORKBOOK

A Framework for Igniting Your Fullest Potential

CONTENTS

Introduction 6

Assessment 8

CHAPTER 1. Personal Freedom 12

CHAPTER 2. Professional Freedom 18

CHAPTER 3. Freedom for Your Family 24

CHAPTER 4. Spiritual Freedom 32

CHAPTER 5. Live What You Believe 38

CHAPTER 6. Live in Purpose 42

CHAPTER 7. Live Your Legacy 46

CHAPTER 8. Going Further, Faster 50

Assessment: Year 1 54

Assessment: Year 3 58

Assessment: Year 5 62

Assessment: Year 10 66

MICHELLE HUBERT

Living With
Purpose

A Framework for Igniting Your Fullest Potential

INTRODUCTION

I'm SO GLAD you're here and have joined me on this journey!

My greatest hope is that during our time together, you'll build a framework that will ignite your fullest potential – allowing you to Live with Purpose!!

In addition to the book, workbook, and these videos, I hope you'll grab a friend to move through this content with. With 8 chapters it would be the perfect 8-week book study to do with someone that you love. Someone who knows you and wants God's best for you.

Reading a chapter on your own, watching the videos, and then spending an hour with a friend reflecting on each chapter and completing the workbook will be transformational.

Just so you know, this is not a "one and done" kind of proposition. It's a journey, a discovery process that takes time.

As we move through the book, workbook, and videos together, don't put pressure on yourself to have this all figured out. If you follow the framework, I'm going to help you accomplish what it's taken me fifteen years to build much more quickly than that.

Although the book and videos will give you context and insight, it's the workbook and more specifically the work you do within the workbook that will create the framework for igniting your fullest potential.

If you haven't completed the assessment, make that a priority soon. Just so you will be in the right frame of mind . . . there should be no judgment, no expectation, it is simply a baseline of where you are today. Trust me, there have been times when I have felt like I was making real progress and times that I feel like I have taken two or three steps back. You are making an investment in yourself. . . . give yourself some love and grace for starting exactly where you are today.

In a perfect world, you would complete this Master Class in eight weeks, but we know the world is rarely if ever perfect. Life gets crazy and demands our full attention from time to time. If you need to skip a week, that's okay, just come right back to our time together as soon as it makes sense for you.

Be patient with yourself, stay with me, repeat the Master Class as necessary, and before you know it, you'll be living with more purpose than you ever could have imagined.

I am honored to be on this journey with you.

—Michelle

ASSESSMENT

> FREEDOM IS NOT ABOUT THE SIZE OF YOUR CAGE, OR THE POWER OF YOUR WINGS, OR NONATTACHMENT TO A PERSON OR A THING. FREEDOM IS ABOUT BEING SO TRULY, MADLY, AND DEEPLY ATTACHED TO YOUR OWN SOUL THAT YOU CAN'T BEAR—IF ONLY FOR A MOMENT—A LIFE THAT DOESN'T HONOR IT.
>
> —Andrea Balt

ASSESS WHERE YOU ARE TODAY AND WHERE YOUR BIGGEST OPPORTUNITY LIES!

At the end of each section put your total number of true answers.

Personal

(T/F) I feel my life is balanced between work, self, job, etc.

(T/F) I know my core beliefs and my "why" – and live in them.

(T/F) I have daily habits that support my health and well-being.

(T/F) I have built healthy boundaries in my personal life.

(T/F) I have a written personal development plan.

TOTAL _____

Family

(T/F) I care more about being present with my family than my family being perfect.

(T/F) My family consistently takes time for planning of fun, quality time, and responsibilities.

(T/F) I am investing time, effort, and energy into the most important relationships in my life.

(T/F) I have built healthy boundaries that support my family success.

(T/F) I have a written family success plan.

TOTAL _____

Professional

(T/F) My current career inspires me and allows me to work in my passion.

(T/F) I have a framework that allows me to operate professionally without chaos.

(T/F) I am not simply surviving in my career – I am thriving.

(T/F) I have built healthy boundaries in my professional life.

(T/F) I have a written professional development plan.

TOTAL _____

Spiritual

(T/F) I have surrendered to the purpose for which I've been called.

(T/F) I have aligned myself with people and resources that continue my spiritual development.

(T/F) I have daily practices that support my well-being and are aligned with my spiritual values.

(T/F) I have built healthy boundaries to support my spiritual success.

(T/F) I have a written spiritual development plan.

TOTAL _____

Utilize your totals to identify where your biggest opportunity lies.

CHAPTER 1

PERSONAL FREEDOM

FEAR IS THE BIGGEST BARRIER TO LIVING COURAGEOUSLY. WE HAVE TO BE UNDENIABLY GROUNDED IN WHO WE ARE AND BECOME THE AUTHORS OF OUR OWN STORY.

READING TIME

As you read Chapter 1: "Personal Freedom" in *Living with Purpose*, reflect on the questions.

REFLECT AND TAKE ACTION:

Do you feel you currently have personal freedom? If not, what is holding you back from attaining it?

_____
_____
_____
_____
_____
_____
_____

What has held you back from personal freedom in the past?

_____
_____
_____
_____
_____
_____
_____

What is your vision for your life?

_____
_____
_____
_____
_____
_____
_____

Use the Personal Values List below to begin your thinking around Personal, Professional, Family, and Spiritual beliefs.

Personal Values List

- AUTHENTICITY
- ACHIEVEMENT
- ADVENTURE
- AUTHORITY
- AUTONOMY
- BALANCE
- BEAUTY
- BOLDNESS
- COMPASSION
- CHALLENGE
- CITIZENSHIP
- COMMUNITY
- COMPETENCY
- CONTRIBUTION
- CREATIVITY
- CURIOSITY
- DETERMINATION
- FAIRNESS
- FAITH
- FAME
- FRIENDSHIPS
- FUN
- GROWTH
- HAPPINESS
- HONESTY
- HUMOR
- INFLUENCE
- INNER HARMONY
- JUSTICE
- KINDNESS
- KNOWLEDGE
- LEADERSHIP
- LEARNING
- LOVE
- LOYALTY
- MEANINGFUL WORK
- OPENNESS
- OPTIMISM
- PEACE
- PLEASURE
- POISE
- POPULARITY
- RECOGNITION
- RELIGION
- REPUTATION
- RESPECT
- RESPONSIBILITY
- SECURITY
- SELF-RESPECT
- SERVICE
- SPIRITUALITY
- STABILITY
- SUCCESS
- STATUS
- TRUSTWORTHINESS
- WEALTH
- WISDOM

What lies about yourself have you believed in the past that you no longer believe?

_____
_____
_____
_____
_____
_____

Are there any lies or limiting beliefs you currently live with?

_____
_____
_____
_____
_____
_____

What is your personal development plan?

Write out your personal mission statement.

Be sure to share your mission statement with your "board of directors."

CHAPTER 2

PROFESSIONAL FREEDOM

REMEMBER, IT'S NEVER SOMETHING BIG THAT MAKES THE BIGGEST IMPACT. IT'S THE ACCUMULATION OF LITTLE THINGS DONE CONSISTENTLY OVER TIME.

READING TIME

As you read Chapter 2: "Professional Freedom" in *Living with Purpose*, reflect on the questions.

REFLECT AND TAKE ACTION:

Do you feel you have professional freedom? Why or why not?

_____
_____
_____
_____
_____
_____

How has your professional life changed since its inception?

_____
_____
_____
_____
_____
_____

Are you enthusiastic about your current position? Given the chance, what would you change?

_____
_____
_____
_____
_____
_____
_____
_____

What professional boundaries have you established?

_____
_____
_____
_____
_____
_____

What are you prioritizing in your current professional life?

_____
_____
_____
_____
_____
_____

Write out your professional development plan.

As you think about how you can proactively resolve conflict, capture some notes in the categories below.

DON'T TAKE THE BAIT:

ASSUME THE BEST:

GET THE FACTS:

ENGAGE ALL PARTIES:

EXTEND SOME GRACE:

CHAPTER 3

FREEDOM FOR YOUR FAMILY

HAPPINESS IS FOUND NOT IN HAVING WHAT YOU WANT BUT WANTING WHAT YOU HAVE.

READING TIME

As you read Chapter 3: "Freedom for Your Family" in *Living with Purpose*, reflect on the questions.

REFLECT AND TAKE ACTION:

In what ways is your family a priority in your life? Would others say the same?

_____
_____
_____
_____
_____
_____

How would you define "Freedom for Your Family" in your own words?

_____
_____
_____
_____
_____
_____

How can you be more fully present with your family?

_____
_____
_____
_____
_____
_____

When evaluating a decision for your family, consider the following...

Do you and your family have any family boundaries? What are they?

_____
_____
_____
_____
_____
_____
_____

What's the motive for saying "yes" to something? Who would it please? What is the cost (time, money, energy, etc.)?

_____
_____
_____
_____
_____
_____
_____
_____

How will your family be impacted by this yes, and how would your family be enriched?

_____
_____
_____
_____
_____
_____
_____
_____

Write out your family development plan.

What action steps can you take today to deepen your family's connection?

_____
_____
_____
_____
_____
_____
_____
_____

Write your family mission or vision statement.

Take a moment to dig a little deeper into the 5 components of love that lasts.

LOVE: LIST SOME LITTLE WAYS YOU SHOW LOVE.

1.

2.

3.

TRUST: WRITE A FEW WAYS YOU CAN DEEPEN TRUST.

1.

2.

3.

Respect: List some ways you can handle things when you don't agree.

1.

2.

3.

Collaboration: Name a few ways you problem solve together.

1.

2.

3.

GRACE: WRITE DOWN HOW YOU SHOW GRACE.

1.

2.

3.

CHAPTER 4

SPIRITUAL FREEDOM

EVERY DAY, WE HAVE A LIMITED NUMBER OF RESOURCES, INCLUDING FAITH. LET'S FIND THE DAILY PRACTICES THAT CAN RENEW AND RESTORE THAT FOR US.

READING TIME

As you read Chapter 4: "Spiritual Freedom" in *Living with Purpose*, reflect on the questions.

REFLECT AND TAKE ACTION:

Do you consider yourself spiritually free?

_____
_____
_____
_____
_____
_____
_____

How do you define spiritual freedom in your own words?

_____
_____
_____
_____
_____
_____
_____

Have you discovered and surrendered to your God-given purpose?

_____
_____
_____
_____
_____
_____
_____

What are your daily practices that keep you grounded and restore your soul?

_____
_____
_____
_____
_____
_____
_____

What spiritual boundaries have you established?

_____
_____
_____
_____
_____
_____
_____
_____

Write out your spiritual development plan.

Write down some ways you can incorporate daily practices to keep you grounded and restore your soul.

Movement

1.

2.

Stillness

1.

2.

Mindset

1.

2.

Creative Pursuits

1.

2.

Service

1.

2.

CHAPTER 5

LIVE WHAT YOU BELIEVE

WHAT IS YOUR LIFE CURRENTLY SAYING ABOUT YOU?

DOES IT REFLECT YOUR VALUES, BELIEFS, AND DREAMS?

READING TIME

As you read Chapter 5: "Live What You Believe" in *Living with Purpose*, reflect on the questions.

REFLECT AND TAKE ACTION:

Living what you believe is not as complicated or daunting as it may seem. There is no need to be overwhelmed or intimidated. It is primarily a discovery process. Resisting the pull to conform to what others believe and who they are; and leaning into what you believe and who you are.

Building your list of beliefs over time, as you recognize or uncover them.

And then working to fully live into them daily. It is as easy at one, two, three:

1. Start paying attention to what you believe. What hits you at your core?

2. Start a list of your beliefs, then consider categorizing them.

3. Review them often, and make daily decisions that keep you living into them.

List the beliefs and values that speak to you, and describe your life.

PERSONAL

1.

2.

3.

4.

FAMILY

1.

2.

3.

4.

Professional

1.
2.
3.
4.

Spiritual

1.
2.
3.
4.

CHAPTER 6

LIVE IN PURPOSE

WHAT FILLS YOUR LIFE WITH PASSION?

ARE YOU LEVERAGING THAT PASSION TO FULFILL YOUR PURPOSE?

READING TIME

As you read Chapter 6: "Live in Purpose" in *Living with Purpose*, reflect on the questions.

REFLECT AND TAKE ACTION:

Our passions lead us to our purpose.

Things that bring us joy, fill us with adrenaline, and break our hearts are indicators of purpose. They make our heart race and cause passion to rise up in us. They create a pull in our hearts that is so strong that we cannot ignore it. Paying attention to what those things are can help us live in purpose.

A great framework for living in purpose includes a few "go to" questions for decision making:

- Will this move me closer to my purpose?
- Will it distract me (or my resources) from my purpose?
- How will it impact the most important people in my life?

We have to create space in our lives for what we're saying are the "most important things" by evaluating 3 categories: How we want to use our time, talent, and treasure.

Time: Create Capacity

Review your calendar – is your time being spent moving towards your purpose? List the items you can say NO to on your calendar so that you can say YES to something that moves you deeper into your purpose.

1.

2.

3.

Talent: Protect Strengths

Review how you are leveraging your strengths – are your talents being spent moving towards your purpose? List the talent requests you can say NO to so that you can say YES to something that moves you deeper into your purpose.

1.

2.

3.

TREASURE: CONSERVE FINANCES

Review your bank statements – are your finances being spent moving towards your purpose? Are you spending on things that are distracting you from your purpose? List the spending you can say NO to financially so that you can say YES to something that moves you deeper into your purpose.

1.
2.
3.

CHAPTER 7

LIVE YOUR LEGACY

WHAT ARE YOU CONTRIBUTING TODAY THAT WILL CREATE YOUR LEGACY? ARE YOU GIFTING YOUR UNIQUE TALENT TO THE WORLD?

READING TIME

As you read Chapter 7: "Live Your Legacy" in *Living with Purpose*, reflect on the questions.

REFLECT AND TAKE ACTION:

Living our legacy is about leveraging our purpose to make the contribution today that only we can make, one that lives on long after we are gone. Consider those who have influenced your life in a positive way, and how they've impacted you personally, professional, with family, or spiritually.

List the person most influential in each area of your life, as well as the accomplishments and qualities that led you to admire them.

Personal

_____

_____

Professional

_____

_____

Family

_____

_____

Spiritual

_____

_____

LIVING WITH PURPOSE: WORKBOOK | 47

Now reflect on how you would like to influence others, and be remembered when you are gone. The questions below can help you organize your thoughts around those accomplishments and qualities you would like to make up your legacy.

Consider the following questions:

- What accomplishments personally and professionally would you want highlighted?

- What would you want your family to be able to say about you?

- What would you want your friends to be able to share?

- What would be missing from your community if you were gone tomorrow?

- What would be said about your generosity with your time, talent, and treasure?

PERSONAL

Family

Professional

Spiritual

CHAPTER 8

GOING FURTHER, FASTER

YOUR NEXT CHAPTER WILL PLAY OUT EITHER BY DEFAULT OR DESIGN.

READING TIME

As you read Chapter 8: "Going Further, Faster" in *Living with Purpose*, reflect on the questions.

REFLECT AND TAKE ACTION:

It is the daily choices we make and the habits we create compounded over time that determines our success or failure. Our next step in living with purpose is actually building the framework, allowing you to move towards freedom.

1. What boundaries do you need to build in each area of your life?

2. What habits do you need to begin in each area of your life?

3. What actions do you need to implement to Live What You Believe, Live in Purpose, and Live Your Legacy?

PERSONAL

Boundaries to Build

Habits to Begin

Actions to Implement

FAMILY

Boundaries to Build

Habits to Begin

Actions to Implement

PROFESSIONAL

Boundaries to Build

Habits to Begin

Actions to Implement

SPIRITUAL

Boundaries to Build

Habits to Begin

Actions to Implement

ASSESSMENT: YEAR 1

ASSESS WHERE YOU ARE TODAY

Personal

(T/F) I feel my life is balanced between work, self, job, etc.

(T/F) I know my core beliefs and my "why" – and live in them.

(T/F) I have daily habits that support my health and well-being.

(T/F) I have built healthy boundaries in my personal life.

(T/F) I have a written personal development plan.

	1st Assessment	Today
TOTAL		

Family

(T/F) I care more about being present with my family than my family being perfect.

(T/F) My family consistently takes time for planning of fun, quality time, and responsibilities.

(T/F) I am investing time, effort, and energy into the most important relationships in my life.

(T/F) I have built healthy boundaries that support my family success.

(T/F) I have a written family success plan.

	1st Assessment	Today
TOTAL		

Professional

(T/F) My current career inspires me and allows me to work in my passion.

(T/F) I have a framework that allows me to operate professionally without chaos.

(T/F) I am not simply surviving in my career – I am thriving.

(T/F) I have built healthy boundaries in my professional life.

(T/F) I have a written professional development plan.

	1st Assessment	Today
TOTAL		

Spiritual

(T/F) I have surrendered to the purpose for which I've been called.

(T/F) I have aligned myself with people and resources that continue my spiritual development.

(T/F) I have daily practices that support my well-being and are aligned with my spiritual values.

(T/F) I have built healthy boundaries to support my spiritual success.

(T/F) I have a written spiritual development plan.

	1st Assessment	Today
TOTAL		

ASSESSMENT: YEAR 3

ASSESS WHERE YOU ARE TODAY

Personal

(T/F) I feel my life is balanced between work, self, job, etc.

(T/F) I know my core beliefs and my "why" – and live in them.

(T/F) I have daily habits that support my health and well-being.

(T/F) I have built healthy boundaries in my personal life.

(T/F) I have a written personal development plan.

	1st Assessment	Year 1	Today
TOTAL			

Family

(T/F) I care more about being present with my family than my family being perfect.

(T/F) My family consistently takes time for planning of fun, quality time, and responsibilities.

(T/F) I am investing time, effort, and energy into the most important relationships in my life.

(T/F) I have built healthy boundaries that support my family success.

(T/F) I have a written family success plan.

	1st Assessment	Year 1	Today
TOTAL			

Professional

(T/F) My current career inspires me and allows me to work in my passion.

(T/F) I have a framework that allows me to operate professionally without chaos.

(T/F) I am not simply surviving in my career – I am thriving.

(T/F) I have built healthy boundaries in my professional life.

(T/F) I have a written professional development plan.

	1st Assessment	Year 1	Today
TOTAL			

Spiritual

(T/F) I have surrendered to the purpose for which I've been called.

(T/F) I have aligned myself with people and resources that continue my spiritual development.

(T/F) I have daily practices that support my well-being and are aligned with my spiritual values.

(T/F) I have built healthy boundaries to support my spiritual success.

(T/F) I have a written spiritual development plan.

	1st Assessment	Year 1	Today
TOTAL			

ASSESSMENT: YEAR 5

ASSESS WHERE YOU ARE TODAY

Personal

(T/F) I feel my life is balanced between work, self, job, etc.

(T/F) I know my core beliefs and my "why" – and live in them.

(T/F) I have daily habits that support my health and well-being.

(T/F) I have built healthy boundaries in my personal life.

(T/F) I have a written personal development plan.

TOTAL	1st	Year 1	Year 3	Today

Family

(T/F) I care more about being present with my family than my family being perfect.

(T/F) My family consistently takes time for planning of fun, quality time, and responsibilities.

(T/F) I am investing time, effort, and energy into the most important relationships in my life.

(T/F) I have built healthy boundaries that support my family success.

(T/F) I have a written family success plan.

TOTAL	1st	Year 1	Year 3	Today

Professional

(T/F) My current career inspires me and allows me to work in my passion.

(T/F) I have a framework that allows me to operate professionally without chaos.

(T/F) I am not simply surviving in my career – I am thriving.

(T/F) I have built healthy boundaries in my professional life.

(T/F) I have a written professional development plan.

	1st	Year 1	Year 3	Today
TOTAL				

Spiritual

(T/F) I have surrendered to the purpose for which I've been called.

(T/F) I have aligned myself with people and resources that continue my spiritual development.

(T/F) I have daily practices that support my well-being and are aligned with my spiritual values.

(T/F) I have built healthy boundaries to support my spiritual success.

(T/F) I have a written spiritual development plan.

	1st	Year 1	Year 3	Today
TOTAL				

ASSESSMENT: YEAR 10

ASSESS WHERE YOU ARE TODAY

Personal

(T/F) I feel my life is balanced between work, self, job, etc.

(T/F) I know my core beliefs and my "why" – and live in them.

(T/F) I have daily habits that support my health and well-being.

(T/F) I have built healthy boundaries in my personal life.

(T/F) I have a written personal development plan.

	1st	Year 1	Year 3	Year 5	Today
TOTAL					

Family

(T/F) I care more about being present with my family than my family being perfect.

(T/F) My family consistently takes time for planning of fun, quality time, and responsibilities.

(T/F) I am investing time, effort, and energy into the most important relationships in my life.

(T/F) I have built healthy boundaries that support my family success.

(T/F) I have a written family success plan.

	1st	Year 1	Year 3	Year 5	Today
TOTAL					

Professional

(T/F) My current career inspires me and allows me to work in my passion.

(T/F) I have a framework that allows me to operate professionally without chaos.

(T/F) I am not simply surviving in my career – I am thriving.

(T/F) I have built healthy boundaries in my professional life.

(T/F) I have a written professional development plan.

	1st	Year 1	Year 3	Year 5	Today
TOTAL					

Spiritual

(T/F) I have surrendered to the purpose for which I've been called.

(T/F) I have aligned myself with people and resources that continue my spiritual development.

(T/F) I have daily practices that support my well-being and are aligned with my spiritual values.

(T/F) I have built healthy boundaries to support my spiritual success.

(T/F) I have a written spiritual development plan.

	1st	Year 1	Year 3	Year 5	Today
TOTAL					

www.ingramcontent.com/pod-product-compliance
Lightning Source LLC
Chambersburg PA
CBHW062122080426
42734CB00012B/2948